Rocks & Minerals
of California

T0166272

Dan R. Lynch
& Bob Lynch

Adventure Quick Guides
YOUR WAY TO EASILY IDENTIFY ROCKS & MINERALS

Adventure Quick Guides

This guide covers 72 of the most common and desirable rocks and minerals in California. In it, you'll learn simple ways to identify your finds, as well as tips to help differentiate them from similar materials. To that end, this book also includes some finds that are commonly misidentified or frequently fool beginners, as well as a few famous California minerals that are too rare for you to collect yourself but that you may still encounter due to their prominence in museums and rock shops.

Helpful notes for using this Quick Guide

- Read the "How to use this guide" section carefully, as it will help novices learn the difference between a rock and a mineral

- The guidelines presented on the following pages consist of the basic knowledge all collectors will need to identify rocks and minerals

- This Quick Guide will work best as a supplement to a more in-depth field guide that covers the specific state or area in which you plan to collect

ABOUT THE AUTHORS

Dan R. Lynch grew up learning the subtle differences between rocks and the nuances of mineral identification firsthand in his parents' rock shop.
Bob Lynch, with wife Nancy, opened that rock shop in 1992, putting to work his stone cutting and polishing skills learned from a lifetime of being a jeweler. Together, Dan and Bob wrote a series of field guides to help readers "decode" the complexities of geology and figure out what exactly they've found.

ALSO FROM AUTHORS DAN R. LYNCH AND BOB LYNCH

Expand your knowledge of rocks & minerals with these top-selling products. They are applicable to California—and the entire contiguous United States.

10 9 8 7 6 5 4 3
Rocks & Minerals of California Quick Guide
Copyright © 2017 by Dan R. Lynch
Published by Adventure Publications
An imprint of AdventureKEEN
310 Garfield Street South
Cambridge, Minnesota 55008
(800) 678-7006
www.adventurepublications.net
All rights reserved. Printed in China.
ISBN 978-1-59193-747-0

Cover design by Jonathan Norberg
Book design by Dan R. Lynch

All photos by Dan R. Lynch
All images copyrighted

How to Use This Guide

If you are new to rock and mineral collecting, or are just a curious traveler wondering about the rocks underfoot, you may not know that every rock and mineral has distinctive identifying traits. Often, determining the identity of a rock or mineral is as simple as trying to scratch it with a pocket knife, or noting how "shiny" it is. And once you've identified what you've collected, you've taken the first step toward being a collector, also known as a "rockhound." This book will teach you the key traits of 72 California rocks and minerals and help you to identify them.

What is the difference between rocks and minerals?

Rocks and minerals are intimately related, yet are quite different. A **mineral** can be thought of as a pure substance and consists of a definite chemical compound. Common table salt, for example, is actually a mineral called halite, which always consists of a chemical compound called sodium chloride. Because of their uniform compositions, minerals **crystallize**, or harden, into very definite shapes. Halite virtually always forms as perfect cubes. **Rocks**, on the other hand, contain a mixture of different minerals. Rocks form in a number of different ways—such as from the cooling of molten rock or the consolidation of sand—but they always appear as masses consisting of grain-like mineral particles, whether they are large or microscopic.

A crystal of calcite, a mineral

A sample of gabbro, a rock

How do I identify a rock?

Studying rocks can get very complicated, and identifying rarer rock types will require you to do lots of research. But the very basic and most abundant kinds of rock can be identified by noting hardness, color, texture, and grain size. A rock's **hardness** can vary, but whether or not a pocket knife will easily scratch a rock will aid in identification. One of the best traits to examine is **grain size**, which is a measure of the size of the mineral grains of which the rock is composed. Granite is an example of a coarse-grained rock, with large, chunky, easily visible mineral grains. And rhyolite is an example of a very fine-grained rock, with mineral grains so small that the rock appears uniform in color. Grain size is generally only used to describe volcanic rocks (formed from the solidification of molten rock), but for the purposes of this book, it will be used to describe the texture of all rocks.

Granite, a coarse-grained rock (actual size)

Diabase, a medium-grained rock (actual size)

Rhyolite, a fine-grained rock (actual size)

How do I identify a mineral?

With thousands of known minerals, telling one apart from another can be daunting. But unlike rocks, minerals have definitive features that are easy to test and examine. Only a handful of minerals are truly considered "common" and easily found by amateurs. To identify these, hardness, color, luster, and crystal shape are very helpful traits to note. The **hardness** of a mineral can be determined by scratching it with a tool, such as a pocket knife or your fingernail. When trying to scratch a mineral, it is important to not apply too much pressure, as this can give you a false result. The tool must easily "bite" into the mineral without high pressure. **Luster**, a measure of how "shiny" a mineral is, is also very helpful to note. For example, some minerals are dull, or barely shiny at all, while many are glassy, or glass-like. Many others are obviously metallic. But it is **crystal shape** that is the most important trait to examine. Minerals form in definitive shapes, so two specimens of the same mineral, even those from different sides of the earth, will share the same shape. Being able to identify a particular mineral's shape is critical to help determine its identity. The exception is when a specimen is broken or when it formed **massively** (with no crystal shape evident, such as when it formed in a tight space). In these cases, you'll have to rely on other characteristics.

A well-formed crystal of dull feldspar

A massive sample of metallic chalcopyrite

Identifying your find

The first step is to determine if you've found a rock or a mineral. Once you've figured that out, go to the appropriate section of the book and compare your rock or mineral to the photos and see if it matches the description that follows. And if you're having a hard time distinguishing your find because two of the minerals look alike (quartz and calcite, say), read the "how are they different" notes, as this will teach you practical ways to differentiate them. If you can't seem to find your specimen in the book, you may have something more uncommon; see the note under "Final Notes."

Is there anything that I can't collect?

Collecting anything in national parks, on Native American reservations, and some (but not all) state parks and forests is illegal. In addition, you'll be trespassing if you collect without permission on privately owned property, so always be aware of where you are collecting and what the rules are.

California also has rules that prohibit collecting vertebrate fossils (fossils of animals with a backbone, such as fish, reptiles, and dinosaurs) due to their scientific importance. It is also illegal to collect Native American artifacts, which should instead be reported to authorities. Familiarize yourself with local and state collecting laws before heading into the field.

Geologic Regions of California

From the dry deserts of its southeast to the wet coasts of its north-west, California is extremely geographically diverse, and it is just as complex geologically. More minerals are found in California than in any other state, making the state a collector's dream. But before you start collecting, you need to understand the state's geographic regions; the map below will help you get a general idea of these areas and what they may hold. In the north, the **Klamath Mountains**, the **Cascade Range**, and the **Modoc Plateau** are regions with lots of volcanic rocks, formed when molten rock hardened either deep within the earth or when it erupted onto the earth's surface. The **Basin and Range** region is similar, containing a mixture of volcanic rocks and metamorphic rocks (rocks that have been changed by pressure and heat). The **Sierra Nevada Range**, the **Coastal Ranges**, and the **Peninsular Ranges** are all mountain chains that contain a great variety of rocks, and all three are lucrative collecting areas. Finally, the **Great Valley** and **Mojave Desert** areas are dry, low-lying regions where the arid environments lead to interesting finds. Throughout this book, we will refer to these general areas to give you a basic indication of where certain materials are found.

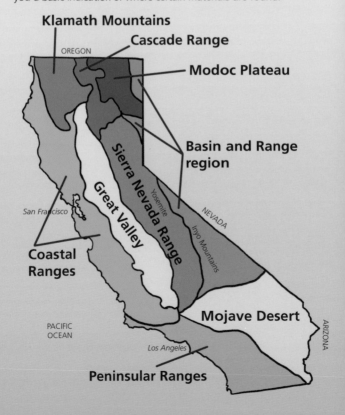

Coarse-grained Rocks

Granite
A very common rock; makes up much of the Sierra Nevadas

- Hard; not typically scratched with a pocket knife
- Dense and coarse-grained with a mottled coloration; gray, yellow, brown, pink, and black
- Contains large, angular, embedded crystals, ranging from glassy to nearly metallic
- Easily found across the state, but particularly prevalent in the Sierra Nevadas and on the coast

How are they different?
Granite is lighter in color than diorite and much more common

Diorite
A common volcanic rock that resembles granite

- Hard; not typically scratched with a pocket knife
- Dense and coarse-grained with a mottled coloration; black, gray, brown and white
- Contains fewer light-colored mineral grains or masses than granite
- Much of the state's diorite is found in the Klamath Mountains and the northern Sierra Nevadas

How are they different?
Diorite is coarser grained and contains more light-colored grains than diabase

Diabase
A dark, dense, medium-grained volcanic rock

- Hard; not typically scratched with a pocket knife
- Dark in color with medium-sized mineral grains, some of which may appear glassy
- Contains small embedded light-colored crystals, sometimes clustered together
- The northern third of the state, particularly in the Klamath Mountains, will yield diabase

How are they different?
Gabbro is much coarser grained and contains much larger embedded crystals

Gabbro
An uncommon dark greenish coarse-grained volcanic rock

- Hard; not typically scratched with a pocket knife
- Dark color, typically nearly black and often with a greenish tint; may contain lighter crystals
- Contains large embedded rectangular crystals that are often very reflective or glassy
- The Klamath Mountains and northern portions of the Sierra Nevada Range produce gabbro

Coarse-grained Rocks

Porphyry
Uncommon rocks containing large, very conspicuous crystals

- Fairly hard, may be scratched with a pocket knife
- Can resemble granite, basalt, or rhyolite, but has well-formed angular crystals embedded within it
- Crystals are often lighter colored and are conspicuous, appearing "out of place"
- Most common in mountainous regions, such as the northwest and northeast

How are they different?
Porphyry contains crystals of fairly uniform size and shape embedded in hard rock

Conglomerate and Breccia
Fairly common rocks consisting of smaller rocks stuck together

- Both rocks vary greatly in hardness
- Conglomerate is a rock consisting of small rounded stones cemented together
- Breccia is similar, but consists of broken, angular rock fragments cemented together
- Both are common on the Pacific Coast, particularly the Coastal Ranges north of Santa Barbara

How are they different?
Sandstone is much more even-grained than either conglomerate or breccia

Sandstone
One of the most common sedimentary rocks

- Soft; can be scratched with a pocket knife
- Composed of cemented sand, so it has a coarse, gritty, sandy texture; sometimes crumbly
- Typically light-colored, but often with darker-colored layers or bands
- Sandstone covers much of the state; look along the Pacific Coast and in southern desert areas

How are they different?
Sandstone is coarser and more widespread; tuff often contains glass fragments

Tuff
A common rock composed of compacted volcanic ash

- Ranges in hardness; often fairly soft
- Light gray to brown in color, often with dark spots; finer grained, sometimes glassy
- Frequently contains small fragments of dark volcanic glass (obsidian) embedded within it
- The volcanic far northeastern corner of the state, as well as the area along the Nevada border, yield tuff

Fine-grained Rocks

Shale
A common, layered sedimentary rock

- Soft; can be scratched with a pocket knife
- Highly layered; layers are often easily split apart with a knife blade
- Fine-grained and typically gray to brown in color; may have fossils embedded between layers
- Shale is very abundant along the Pacific Coast and Coastal Ranges, particularly at road cuts

 How are they different?
Shale and mudstone are very similar, but shale is highly layered; mudstone is not

Mudstone
A common, soft sedimentary rock with no layering

- Very soft; easily scratched with a pocket knife
- Resembles shale in most ways but is not layered
- Extremely fine-grained with typically even coloration; usually gray to tan or brown
- Like shale, mudstone is abundant in much of the state, particularly along the Pacific Coast

 How are they different?
Limestone is harder, more widespread, and often lighter in color

Limestone
A very common, light-colored sedimentary rock

- Soft; can be scratched with a pocket knife
- Usually light-colored, gray to brown, sometimes with layers of varying color; has a gritty texture
- Consists primarily of calcite, so it will "fizz" in strong vinegar; sometimes has crystal-lined holes
- Limestone is widespread, especially in the Coastal Ranges and in the San Francisco area

 How are they different?
Travertine is more scarce and is often more porous and/or more translucent

Travertine
A chemically deposited often porous variety of limestone

- Soft; can be scratched with a pocket knife
- Generally light gray to tan or brown; often layered with varying colors
- Forms around hot springs; most travertine is porous, but it can also be translucent and fibrous
- Volcanic areas, such as the state's far northeastern corner and the Yosemite area, produce travertine

Fine-grained Rocks

Rhyolite
A common hard, fine-grained volcanic rock

- Very hard; can't be scratched with a pocket knife
- Fine-grained and light-colored, often in shades of gray, brown or reddish
- May have parallel banding, veins of minerals, or many gas bubbles (called pumice)
- Rhyolite is abundant in the Modoc Plateau and northern Sierra Nevada Range

How are they different?
Basalt is always darker than rhyolite; basalt typically doesn't show any banding

Basalt
A common, dark and dense volcanic rock

- Fairly hard; may be scratched with a pocket knife with some effort
- Very fine-grained and always dark in color, from gray to greenish black, occasionally reddish
- Often contains bubble-shaped cavities
- The Modoc Plateau and northern Sierra Nevada Range areas produce much of the state's basalt

How are they different?
Chert is far harder, more brittle, and has a waxy look on a fresh break

Chert
A very common and extremely hard, waxy-looking rock

- Very hard; can't be scratched with a pocket knife
- Typically light gray to brown or black; always opaque; sometimes with colored bands
- Brittle; breaks into very sharp-edged pieces; worn pieces can appear smooth, as if polished
- Chert turns up on any beach or river as worn pebbles, especially along the Pacific Coast

How are they different?
Obsidian is extremely glassy in appearance; chert is more opaque and common

Obsidian
An uncommon black, translucent, shiny volcanic glass

- Hard; not typically scratched with a pocket knife
- Very brittle, glassy and dark, typically black or dark brown in color; translucent when thin
- Breaks in circular shapes when struck; broken fragments have extremely sharp edges
- The Yosemite area, the Coastal Ranges, and the Modoc Plateau all produce obsidian

Fine-grained Rocks

Schist
Common, dense and highly layered metamorphic rocks

- Fairly hard; most types can be scratched with a pocket knife with some effort
- Dense and highly layered; typically gray and may contain countless tiny shiny flecks
- May contain very hard crystals, like garnets
- Schists are common in mountainous areas, particularly in the Sierra Nevadas and the Peninsular Ranges

 How are they different?
Schist contains much more compact layers and is often "glittery" with shiny grains

Gneiss
Gneiss (pronounced "nice") is a common metamorphic rock

- Fairly hard; may be scratched with a pocket knife
- Layered with bands of varying color; layers may be differentiated by coarser or finer mineral grains
- Resembles other rocks, particularly granite, but in a layered form
- The Coastal and Peninsular Ranges produce a lot of gneiss

 How are they different?
Quartzite is glassier and more uniform in texture and hardness

Quartzite
A common, extremely hard and dense metamorphic rock

- Very hard; can't be scratched with a pocket knife
- Generally light in color, often with faint layering, and typically translucent, especially when thin
- Grainy and glassy when freshly broken; smooth and dull when weathered; sometimes banded
- Quartzite is easily found on Pacific Coast beaches and in Yosemite area rivers

 How are they different?
Marble is softer and typically does not exhibit layering; quartzite is more common

Marble
An uncommon metamorphic rock formed from limestone

- Soft; easily scratched with a pocket knife
- Often exhibits light coloration, sometimes pure white, occasionally dark; virtually always opaque
- Large, glassy grains often present; marble will also "fizz" in strong vinegar
- Marble occurs sparingly in the Basin and Range region, as well as in the Coastal Ranges

Dull to Glassy Minerals

Quartz
The most common mineral; found in every environment

- Very hard; can't be scratched with a pocket knife
- Light-colored (typically colorless to white), glassy, and translucent; breaks in circular shapes
- Crystals have six sides and a pointed tip; masses are more common, often found loose as pebbles or embedded in rocks like granite
- Any beach or river will yield pebbles

 How are they different?
Quartz is much, much harder than calcite; calcite breaks more readily

Calcite
A very common mineral, particularly in sedimentary rocks

- Soft; easily scratched with a pocket knife
- Light-colored (typically colorless to white), translucent, and often glassy
- Forms crystals shaped as steep six-sided points or blocky "leaning" cubes; will "fizz" in vinegar
- Calcite is widespread, especially in sedimentary regions such as in central and southern California

 How are they different?
Dolomite is less common than calcite and its crystals tend to be more opaque

Dolomite
A common mineral typically found in limestone

- Soft; easily scratched with a pocket knife
- Light-colored with a pearly luster; sometimes translucent, but more often opaque
- Crystals form as clusters of blocky or bladed shapes, often with curved or rounded faces
- Limestone-rich regions, such as the Coastal Ranges, north of San Francisco, include a lot of dolomite

 How are they different?
Gypsum is far softer than dolomite and will dissolve very slowly in warm water

Gypsum
A common and extremely soft mineral

- Very soft; easily scratched with your fingernail
- Light-colored, typically white to tan; may appear glassy, fibrous, or grainy
- Forms elongated needle-like crystals, or as masses in rock; will slowly dissolve in warm water
- Gypsum is best found in dry areas, like in the Death Valley region and along the Nevada border

Dull to Glassy Minerals

Baryte (Barite)
A soft mineral so dense that even small pieces feel heavy

- Soft; easily scratched with a pocket knife
- Light-colored, translucent, and often glassy; very brittle and breaks easily
- Often found as blades grown in nearly parallel clusters; specimens will feel heavy for their size
- Baryte is not rare and turns up in rock cavities in the Klamath and Inyo Mountain Ranges

 How are they different?
A piece of baryte has more "heft" than any similarly sized piece of fluorite

Fluorite
A fairly common mineral found in a rainbow of colors

- Soft; easily scratched with a pocket knife
- Varies in color, often white, green, purple, or blue; typically glassy and translucent
- Crystals are often shaped like cubes or octahedrons; also as irregular or lumpy masses
- Fluorite is found in the eastern portion of the state, from the Inyo Mountains to the Mojave

 How are they different?
Olivine is far harder and generally yellow-green in color; fluorite is scarcer

Olivine
A hard mineral most common as grains in dark rocks

- Hard; can't be scratched with a pocket knife
- Typically greenish yellow in color and very glassy and translucent
- Most often found as small embedded grains in dark rocks like gabbro; also found loose in sand
- Dark igneous rocks, such as those in the Klamath and Cascade Ranges, often host olivine

 How are they different?
Sulfur is far softer and much rarer

Sulfur
A rare native element found in volcanic areas

- Very soft; easily scratched with your fingernail
- Always lemon-yellow to dark yellow; translucent when crystallized; crusts are often opaque
- Forms as wedge-shaped crystals, but more commonly found as irregular masses or crusts on rock
- Sulfur is rare; it can be found in the Death Valley region and in the northern Coastal Ranges

Dull to Glassy Minerals

Feldspar group
The most abundant family of minerals; found in many rocks

- Hard; can't be scratched with a pocket knife
- Light-colored; often white, gray, or pink (rarely colorless); typically opaque or slightly translucent
- Most commonly found embedded in rocks like granite as blocky, angular grains or masses
- Various feldspars can be found all across California; the Yosemite area produces large crystals

How are they different?
Feldspars are far more common and tend to be lighter in color than pyroxenes

Pyroxene group
A very common group of minerals found in dark rocks

- Very hard; can't be scratched with a pocket knife
- Generally dark-colored minerals, often brown to black; frequently lustrous and glassy
- Most pyroxenes are found as blocky or needle-like grains in volcanic rocks, particularly gabbro
- They are found all over, but the Klamath and Cascade Ranges can produce large crystals

How are they different?
While very similar, amphiboles tend to be more fibrous and may be lighter in color

Amphibole group
A common family easily confused with the pyroxenes

- Hard; can't be scratched with a pocket knife
- Often fairly dark-colored minerals, light to dark brown or black; often fibrous or "silky" in luster
- Most amphiboles are found as blocky embedded grains in rocks, particularly granite or rhyolite
- Amphibole minerals are abundant; the granite in the Yosemite region contains large crystals

How are they different?
Zeolites are found as tiny crystals in cavities, not usually as part of the rock itself

Scale = 2x actual size

Scale = 2x actual size

Zeolite group
A common family of minerals formed in weathering rocks

- Soft; can be scratched with a pocket knife
- A light-colored mineral group; often colorless to white or gray, and typically always glassy
- Zeolites form as tiny blocky or needle-like crystal clusters within cavities in dark rocks like basalt
- Zeolites are best found in volcanic rocks; look in the northernmost third of the state

Dull to Glassy Minerals

Turquoise
A rare but very popular copper-bearing mineral

- Fairly hard; may be scratched with a pocket knife with some effort
- Blue-green and opaque, typically with a dull luster
- Generally forms as irregular masses or veins within cavities or cracks in rock
- Turquoise is very scarce; look in desert regions like the Mojave Desert along the Nevada border

 How are they different?
Chrysocolla is far more common and widespread, but is also much softer

Chrysocolla
A soft and common mineral that forms when copper weathers

- Soft; easily scratched with a pocket knife
- Pale blue to bluish green in color, often growing on or with other copper-bearing minerals
- Typically forms as a thin powdery crust or coating; also can occur as veins or masses in rock
- Crusts of chrysocolla are most abundant in dry areas, such as along the southern Nevada border

 How are they different?
Malachite is harder and exhibits a fibrous structure; chrysocolla is often crumbly

Malachite
An attractive and somewhat common copper mineral

- Soft; can be scratched with a pocket knife
- Vivid green in color; sometimes exhibits banding on edges or on cross-sections
- Forms as lumpy or fibrous masses or crusts on or near other copper minerals; rarely as hair-like crystals
- Look in desert regions, particularly the Mojave Desert along the Arizona border

 How are they different?
Epidote is much harder and a bit more common; epidote is more yellow-green

Epidote
An uncommon mineral with distinctive color

- Very hard; can't be scratched with a pocket knife
- Virtually always a distinctive yellow-green or pistachio-green color, though can be browner
- Crystals are elongated with grooved sides; more common as opaque crusts, masses or veins
- Epidote is found in mountainous regions or along rivers, especially in the southern half of the state

Dull to Glassy Minerals

Jade
A favored green gemstone collected for centuries

- Fairly hard; may be scratched with a pocket knife
- Light to dark green in color, sometimes with gray or brown mottling and a "greasy" luster
- Found as irregular masses, often as rounded pebbles on coastal beaches
- Jade is found on Pacific Coast beaches, as well as along rivers in the Klamath Mountains

How are they different?
Jade is harder and scarcer; serpentines are not as frequently found on beaches

Serpentine group
A fairly common group of soft, "greasy" minerals

- Soft; easily scratched with a pocket knife
- Green to yellow or brown and typically opaque
- Forms as irregular masses, often with parallel grooves and a "greasy" feel; rarer serpentines appear as bundles of parallel fibers
- The Klamath Mountains, Coastal Ranges, and San Francisco Bay areas are lucrative areas

How are they different?
Serpentine minerals are harder than talc; talc can be scratched with your fingernail

Talc
Talc is the softest mineral, though it's somewhat uncommon

- Extremely soft; easily scratched with your fingernail
- Light-colored, white to pale green, and opaque, sometimes with a tan, weathered exterior
- Forms as irregular flaky masses that are chalky and feel like soap
- Talc is found along the Sierra Nevada and Inyo Mountain Ranges, both at outcrops and in mines

How are they different?
Talc is lighter in color and forms as large masses rather than tiny crystals or crusts

Chlorite group
Very common, very soft minerals found coating rock cavities

- Very soft; easily scratched with your fingernail
- Dark-colored in shades of green or brown, appearing "greasy" in luster
- Forms as thin coatings or tiny six-sided crystals within cavities in rock, particularly in basalt
- The Klamath Mountains and the Cascade Range produce chlorites in weathered rocks

Dull to Glassy Minerals

Opal
A common glassy material that does not form crystals

- Fairly hard; may be scratched with a pocket knife
- Glass-like; light-colored, often white and opaque
- Does not form crystals; typically found as veins or pockets in volcanic rocks, such as obsidian, or around hot springs as crusts and masses
- Found in the Modoc Plateau and Basin and Range areas, or in the Yosemite area

How are they different?
Opal is slightly softer and often lighter in color; jasper is not so glass-like

Jasper
The very common and colorful variety of chert

- Hard; not scratched with a pocket knife
- Found in any color, though typically brown to red, and often mottled; opaque unless very thin
- Forms as veins or pockets in rock; often found as loose waxy rounded pebbles
- Extremely abundant along the Pacific Coast and virtually any river in the state

How are they different?
Jasper is always more opaque than chalcedony under bright light

Chalcedony
A very common variety of dense, compact quartz

- Hard; cannot be scratched with a pocket knife
- Color can vary greatly, but red to brown or gray is most common; often mottled or banded
- Forms as pockets or veins in rocks; often found as loose, waxy, translucent rounded pebbles
- Very abundant along the Pacific Coast and found in almost any river, particularly in low-lying regions

How are they different?
Chalcedony's color is often mottled while agates are organized in ring-like bands

Agates
Uncommon banded gemstones of mysterious formation

- Hard; cannot be scratched with a pocket knife
- Color varies greatly; multicolored in concentric rings, typically in shades of red, brown, or gray
- Found as waxy colorful pebbles in rivers or gravel, often with a rough exterior
- Agates are found in many locales in the Mojave Desert and elsewhere in southeastern California

Dull to Glassy Minerals

Beryl
This rare mineral is best known for its green variety, emerald

- Very hard; can't be scratched with a pocket knife
- Typically light-colored, often white or gray, sometimes blue (aquamarine) or green (emerald)
- Forms as glassy, elongated, six-sided crystals in coarse-grained rocks, such as granite
- The Peninsular Ranges, particularly near Pala, northwest of San Diego, produce crystals

How are they different?
Corundum is harder and its crystals often have tapered, pointed ends

Corundum
Rare and desirable, pink corundum is better known as ruby

- Very hard; can't be scratched with a pocket knife
- Often gray to bluish (sapphire) or pink (ruby) in color, and usually glassy in luster
- Forms as short, stubby six-sided crystals, often with tapered ends; found in coarse rocks
- The Peninsular Ranges, east of Los Angeles, produce much of the state's rubies

How are they different?
Corundum is much harder; tourmalines are more common

Tourmaline group
A fairly uncommon group of attractive minerals

- Very hard; can't be scratched with a pocket knife
- Most tourmalines are black, glassy, and opaque; a rarer variety is pink or green and translucent
- Crystals are slender and elongated with striated (grooved) sides and a triangular cross-section
- The Peninsular Ranges are known for tourmalines from mines and outcrops

How are they different?
Tourmalines are elongated, while garnets are ball-like; garnets are more common

Garnet group
A common family of very hard, colorful minerals

- Very hard; can't be scratched with a pocket knife
- Garnets are most commonly red to brown or black, rarely green; translucent and glassy
- Crystals appear as faceted "balls," often embedded in schist or granite; also can be found loose
- Garnets are widespread; look in the Klamath Mountains, the Sierra Nevadas, and along the Pacific Coast

Dull to Glassy Minerals

Howlite
An unusual mineral found at just a few California locations

- Fairly soft; can be scratched with a pocket knife
- Generally always gray on their rough exterior, and white in the chalky, dull interior
- Found as cauliflower-like rounded masses, typically freed of its host rock
- Abundant in the Los Angeles area, particularly around Tick Canyon, but rare elsewhere

How are they different?
Howlite does not form crystals, nor is it ever translucent

Halite
Common table salt in its natural form

- Very soft; easily scratched with your fingernail
- Colorless to white or pink; typically translucent and glassy, but opaque when poorly formed
- Forms as cubic crystals, often grown together in complex shapes; easily dissolves in water
- Look in the Searles and Mono Lake areas, or in the Death Valley and Great Valley regions

How are they different?
Halite's crystals are cubic while hanksite's are hexagonal; halite is more common

Hanksite
A rare mineral formed when ancient seas evaporated

- Soft; easily scratched with a pocket knife
- Colorless to white or gray; typically translucent and fairly glassy in luster
- Develops hexagonal (six-sided) crystals with tapered ends; also dissolves in water
- The Searles and Mono Lake areas are among the only places to find this rare California mineral

How are they different?
Ulexite is typically very fibrous and is not found as hexagonal crystals

Ulexite
An interesting mineral found only in arid regions

- Soft; can be scratched with your fingernail
- Colorless to white and typically translucent; often glassy but also frequently fibrous and flaky
- Found as irregular masses as well as bundles of parallel fibers with a silky sheen
- The Searles Lake and Death Valley regions are best for finding this rare mineral; look in salt flats

Metallic Minerals

Hematite
The most common iron-bearing mineral

- Fairly hard; may be scratched with a pocket knife
- Metallic-gray in color, turning rusty red when weathered or powdered
- Takes a variety of forms, occurring as crusts on rock, lumpy rounded masses, or thin blades
- Hematite is abundant and most common as reddish stains; it is found virtually anywhere

How are they different?
Hematite turns reddish when crushed and powdered; goethite turns yellow-brown

Goethite
Goethite (pronounced "ger-tite") is a common iron mineral

- Fairly hard; barely scratched with a pocket knife
- Metallic black in color; often coated in a dusty orange- or yellow-brown material (limonite)
- Forms as lumpy rounded masses with a fibrous cross-section, or as thin rusty brown crusts
- Goethite can be found nearly anywhere, particularly in mountainous or desert regions

How are they different?
Goethite is not magnetic and will not attract a magnet like magnetite will

Magnetite
A common iron mineral that is strongly magnetic

- Fairly hard; not easily scratched by a pocket knife
- Black and metallic; will strongly attract a magnet
- Takes the form of octahedrons (crystals that resemble two pyramids placed bottom-to-bottom) or as irregular shiny to dull metallic masses
- Magnetite is widespread, particularly in volcanic rocks like those of the Klamath Mountains

How are they different?
Magnetite is magnetic; any piece of galena is very heavy for its size

Galena
The primary ore of lead, galena is heavy and fairly common

- Very soft; easily scratched with a pocket knife
- Gray to bluish gray in color and highly metallic, particularly on a freshly broken surface
- Breaks into perfect cubes; it is very dense and even a small piece will be very heavy for its size
- The southern Sierra Nevadas and the Basin and Range region yield galena in sedimentary rocks

Metallic Minerals

Sphalerite
An uncommon ore of zinc that forms complex crystals

- Soft; easily scratched with a pocket knife
- Typically dark colored and brightly lustrous; ranges from dark red to deep yellow or black
- Crystals are complex in shape, often with triangular features; masses may have a velvety sheen
- Sphalerite is scarce, but the Inyo Mountains and the Death Valley area have produced specimens

How are they different?
Sphalerite is darker, often reddish, and doesn't form as cubes

Pyrite
"Fool's gold" is one of the most common metallic minerals

- Very hard; can't be scratched with a pocket knife
- Brassy yellow in color and very lustrous; sometimes coated in a dull brown rust-like material
- Develops as cube-shaped crystals that are often embedded in rocks; it is very brittle
- Pyrite is very common and found all over the state; look in rivers in mountainous areas

How are they different?
Chalcopyrite is softer than pyrite and does not form cubic crystals

Chalcopyrite
A fairly common copper-bearing metallic mineral

- Soft; easily scratched with a pocket knife
- Brass-like in color, often with an orange tint or a bluish multicolored surface coating
- Most often found as brittle, brightly metallic veins embedded in rocks or quartz
- Not as common as pyrite, but found in similar places; look in mountainous areas

How are they different?
Mica minerals are much softer, are not actually metallic, and form as flaky crystals

Mica group
Mica minerals are a very common constituent of rocks

- Very soft; easily scratched with your fingernail
- Often dark-colored and typically so shiny that it almost appears metallic; not actually metallic
- Crystals form as flexible paper-thin flakes grown in stacks, typically within rocks like granite
- Found everywhere, most often in rocks where it appears as tiny flecks of "glitter," especially in schists

Fossils and Fossil-like

Animal fossils
Preserved remains of ancient animals within rock

- Traces of animals, especially clams, snails, teeth, or coral, embedded in rock
- Most fossils are found in shale or limestone
- Fossils are often colored nearly identically to the rock in which they are embedded
- Generally hard to find statewide, but shellfish fossils are common on the northern Pacific Coast

Dendrites
Plant-like mineral formations on rocks; not actually fossils

- Dendrites are tiny tree-shaped mineral stains formed within cracks and crevices in rocks
- May be black, red-brown, or yellow, depending on the mineral that comprises them
- Microscopically thin; may be easily scratched away
- Found nearly anywhere; look in desert regions such as the Mojave

 How are they different?
Dendrites are extremely thin and can be rubbed away with your fingers

Plant fossils/Petrified wood
Preserved remains of ancient plants within rock

- Impressions of plants, especially leaves, twigs, and ferns, embedded in rock, especially shale
- Quite hard and exhibits all the traits of wood: bark, grain, and rings
- Color can vary from gray to brown to multicolored
- Look in the Mojave Desert, the Coastal Ranges and the Great Valley

 How are they different?
Tufa can look branch-like, but it is lumpy, crumbly, and found freestanding

Tufa
Soft rocky formations found in and around saline lakes

- Very soft; easily scratched with a pocket knife
- Tufa is a variety of limestone formed when calcite precipitates out of surface water
- Formations range from enormous mounds to slender branch-like tubes with lumpy, rough exteriors
- Tufa forms around hot springs and saline (salty) lakes; Mono Lake produces lots of tufa

Commonly Misidentified Minerals

Gold
Gold is a very rare precious metal, sought by many

- Gold is very soft, easily scratched with a knife, and is malleable (bendable)
- Gold is always brightly metallic yellow
- People mistake pyrite and chalcopyrite for gold due to their similar color; both are far harder and brittle
- Most gold is found as minuscule grains in rivers, especially in western California's mountains

Scale = 4x actual size

Scale = 2x actual size

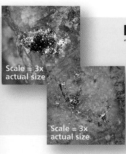

Mercury
"Quicksilver" is a very rare, toxic metal found as a liquid

- A native element and naturally found as a liquid
- Always silvery white and brightly lustrous; often found with a bright red mineral (cinnabar)
- Found as tiny droplets within cavities in rock from mines; not typically found on the surface
- Mercury is very rare but famous from California; found in Sonoma County north of Santa Rosa

Scale = 3x actual size

Scale = 3x actual size

Meteorite
The vast majority of "meteorites" are actually magnetite

- Meteorites fall from space and can be found anywhere but are extremely rare
- Metal-rich meteorites are often magnetic, silver-gray, and have a rough, dark rusty outer crust
- Magnetite, due to its magnetism, is often mistaken for a metallic meteorite; assume a metallic specimen is magnetite unless verified by an expert!

Slag
A waste byproduct of ore processing and industry

- Slag is often dark, glassy to metallic in appearance, and a piece can be heavy for its size
- Colorful slag glass is often mistaken for other rarer minerals, especially opal
- Slag typically has many round bubbles trapped within it (not a trait seen in minerals)
- Some slag appears "melted," as if it had flowed

California Rarities

Benitoite
California's rare and valuable state gem

- Hard; cannot be scratched with a pocket knife
- Light to dark blue or gray-blue; translucent and glassy, opaque if poorly formed
- Develops as triangular-shaped crystals embedded in softer material, often alongside neptunite
- Benitoite is extremely rare and can't be found by amateurs; it is mined near San Benito Mountain

Neptunite
A very rare mineral found with benitoite

- Hard; can be scratched with a pocket knife with some effort
- Always dark, nearly black with a reddish tint; usually nearly opaque and always very glassy
- Forms elongated blocky crystals with angular tips; found alongside benitoite
- Extremely rare; found only at San Benito Mountain

Realgar
A vividly colored ore of arsenic once used as a pigment

- Very soft; easily scratched with a pocket knife
- Brightly colored in shades of orange to red; usually glassy but can be chalky when poorly formed
- Crystals are tiny elongated needles; more commonly found as masses or veins in other minerals
- Realgar is fairly rare, found in quantity only in Kern and San Bernardino County mines

 How are they different?
Realgar is softer; cinnabar is slightly more common and found as larger masses

Cinnabar
An extremely vibrant, colorful mercury-bearing mineral

- Soft; easily scratched with a pocket knife
- Vividly colored in shades of red; glassy to nearly metallic in luster
- Forms most often as masses or veins in rocks such as chert, frequently with tiny drops of mercury
- Mines in the Mayacamas Mountains north of Santa Rosa have produced large amounts

Final Notes

I can't find my specimen in the book. Does that mean it's rare?
Not likely. Many rocks and minerals are considered "common"; the ones represented here are simply among the most abundant. In fact, this book covers perhaps 90 percent of the materials a beginning collector will easily find and identify. So, while you could very well have found something a bit more uncommon than most rocks or minerals, it is more likely that weathering or staining has altered the appearance or hardness of a more common variety. This can make it no longer appear quite as it "should," which can be confusing for beginners.

Some minerals are so much easier to find than others for a variety of reasons. First, it may be extremely abundant. Quartz and calcite, for example, are among the most common minerals, and both can be found in the vast majority of environments, even in places where weathering may quickly destroy soft minerals. Second, the places where most people look for minerals—the beach, a mountainside, a rocky road or riverbed, etc.—are very tough on minerals, and not every specimen will survive. Only the hardest minerals, such as quartz or jasper, will withstand the elements while the other materials around them weather away. This makes them easy to find and very common. Between natural abundance and resistance to weathering, certain rocks and minerals seem to be ubiquitous anywhere you go in California. Some minerals were not included in this book because, although common, they are typically only seen as grains embedded within rocks rather than as loose and collectible specimens. But if you still think you've found something rare, then your next step is further research. Use only the information available to you, such as the specimen's hardness, crystal shape, and where you found it, and don't let wishful thinking cloud the identification process.

What are the best places to look for rocks and minerals?
The best places to find rocks and minerals are wild, natural places where rocks are exposed. Beaches, rivers, and washes (dried-up, seasonal rivers) are excellent places to start looking, as are mountainsides and deserts. Man-made exposures of rock and gravel are extremely lucrative as well; examples include gravel pits, quarries, mine sites, road cuts, and dirt roads. However, these are often dangerous and/or private property, so before venturing out, be sure you're on public land or have obtained proper permission, and make sure you have the proper experience and equipment and are aware of potential wildlife hazards (snakes, scorpions, cacti, etc.).

How should I prepare for going out to collect?
No matter where you're going or for how long, water is essential, as is a cell phone and a GPS system to find your way back. A bucket or backpack is useful to carry specimens, and a camera and magnifier will always be handy. If you have plans to break rock, you'll need thick leather gloves, a rock hammer (not a nail hammer!), and eye protection. Tissues or paper towels are great to protect fragile specimens, as well. Wherever you're headed, always let someone know where you're going, and exercise caution at all times!

Glossary

Arid: Very dry regions, receiving very little rain

Band: An easily identified layer of a differing color within a rock or mineral

Crystal: A solid body with a repeating atomic structure formed when an element or chemical compound solidifies

Facet: An angular side or face of a crystal

Igneous rock: Rock formed from the cooling and solidification of molten rock material originating from beneath the earth's crust

Malleable: Pliable; easily bent

Mass: A mineral formation lacking an obvious crystal shape

Metamorphic rock: Rock formed from the heating and/or compression of older rocks; metamorphic rocks often exhibit layered or warped features

Mineral: A naturally occurring chemical compound or native element that solidifies with a definite internal crystal structure

Native element: An element found naturally uncombined with any other elements, e.g. copper

Octahedron: A three-dimensional structure with eight faces, resembling two pyramids placed base-to-base

Rock: A massive aggregate of mineral grains

Saline: Refers to a mineral-forming environment rich with salt, particularly certain lakes

Sedimentary rock: Rock formed when sediment is cemented together; a region in which sedimentary rocks are predominant is referred to as sedimentary

Vein: A mineral, often a metal, that has filled a crack or similar opening in a host rock or mineral

Volcanic rock: See igneous rock

Widespread: Found in many places, though not necessarily abundant or common

Recommended Reading

Bonewitz, Ronald Louis. *Smithsonian Rock and Gem*. New York: DK Publishing, 2005.

Chesteman, Charles W. *The Audubon Society Field Guide to North American Rocks and Minerals*. New York: Knopf, 1979.

Lynch, Dan R., and Bob Lynch. *The Wonder of North American Agates*. Cambridge: Adventure Publications, 2013.

Mottana, Annibale, et al. *Simon & Schuster's Guide to Rocks and Minerals*. New York: Simon & Schuster, 1978.

Pough, Frederick H. *Rocks and Minerals*. Boston: Houghton Mifflin, 1988.

Robinson, George W. *Minerals*. New York: Simon & Schuster, 1994.

Only Rocks & Minerals Found in California

Organized by rocks/minerals, then by appearance, for quick and easy identification

Simple and convenient—narrow your choices by group, and view just a few photos at a time

- Pocket-size format—easier than laminated foldouts
- Professional photos showing key traits
- Tips for identifying rocks and minerals
- "How are they different?" notes that contrast similar specimens

Get these *Adventure Quick Guides* for your area

ISBN 978-1-59193-747-0

U.S. $9.95

5 0 9 9 5

9 781591 937470

Adventure
PUBLICATIONS
an imprint of AdventureKEEN

NATURE/ROCKS & MINERALS